JAN 1 1 2022

D0606400

JAN 1 1 2022

Pacific Wilderness

Pacific Wilderness

J.A. KRAULIS

GALLERY BOOKS
An Imprint of W. H. Smith Publishers Inc.
112 Madison Avenue
New York City 10016

© 1989 Discovery Books
All rights reserved.

Produced by Discovery Books for:

Gallery Books
An imprint of W.H. Smith Publishers Inc.
112 Madison Avenue
New York, New York 10016

ISBN: 0-8317-6716-2

Design: Denise Maxwell

Printed and bound in Italy

FRONTISPIECE:
*Tide pools and wave-carved rocks at sunset,
Samuel H. Boardman State Park, Oregon.*

CONTENTS

Pacific Coast........ 7

Restless Sea 11

Suspect Terrain.... 53

Redwoods and
Salmon 101

PACIFIC COAST

Different worlds fuse at the edge of a continent. Here, stone and water, earth and ocean collide. Dramatic topography brings the landscape's mosaic alive to meet a shining, undulating expanse of sea that stretches toward a distant horizon, the pure curve of the earth itself. Animals living on the surface of one world struggle to adapt to constraints of gravity, weather and terrain. Different forms of life evolve within the other, watery world, floating unrestrained by earthbound limitations. Some creatures move freely between land and water.

The wilderness fringes bound by the edges of the land, the edges of the sea, are special places. And of all the coasts on earth, perhaps no more spectacular meeting of these worlds exists than along the western margin of North America, from the tip of the Baja Peninsula to the Gulf of Alaska and the Aleutian Islands. Here the desert, the forest and the mountains in turn meet the ocean, and each still thrives, though in ever diminishing havens, in its original, wild state.

The Baja Peninsula belongs to the desert. In some places, the sun broils barren sand dunes, and rain may not fall for twelve months at a time; yet this long, narrow peninsula is renowned for its exotic assemblage of desert plants.

Northward, the coastal climate becomes progressively more humid. Southern-most California gets a bit too much rain for desert and not quite enough for forest, and the vegetation is chaparral, a mix of woody bushes and scrub oak. Around Big Sur, whose long, steep slopes descend in runs down to the sea, are pockets of thick forest. Here is the southern limit of the mists that keep much of the Californian coast moist and cool in summer, and consequently here too are the southernmost stands of redwood, the majestic trees that grow tallest farther north, towards Oregon.

From the redwoods to Alaska, several other species of great trees adorn the Pacific wilderness—Port Orford cedar, western red cedar, western hemlock, Sitka spruce and Douglas fir—the lofty fabric of some of the most impressive forests to be found still standing in the world.

North of the last redwoods, mist gives way to rain. On the Olympic Peninsula in Washington, moss-smothered forest thrives in the rainiest place on the continent, where fifteen feet of precipitation may fall in a year.

The rainforest continues north through British Columbia and the Alaska pan-handle, but at the Olympic Peninsula, the character of the coast begins to change significantly. From Santa Barbara to Cape Flattery, Washington, there is not a single

OPPOSITE:
Numerous streams cascade through the Qualicum
Park of Vancouver Island in British Columbia.

substantial island off the mainland, only sea stacks and rocky islets. The Channel Islands lie off Santa Barbara, and a number of islands flank the Baja Peninsula, but here too almost the entire coastline fronts on the open Pacific. The Strait of Juan de Fuca, however, marks the start of a broken, crenellated coastline, a complex network of passageways and inlets behind and between island archipelagos, running north to the sixtieth parallel.

Glaciers grind to within thirty miles of the sea in the Olympic Mountains. Most of the Pacific coast is rugged. But while mountains of the Baja are snowy in winter and reach ten thousand feet—significantly higher than the Olympics—it is from this corner of Washington northward that true alpine landscape begins to approach within a few miles of salt water.

The high icefields and glaciers of the Coast Mountains in British Columbia tower over long inlets of the sea. In the Alaska Panhandle, some glaciers reach tidewater. Ice-swelled rivers many miles wide and dozens of miles long discard hundreds of small icebergs into the inlets of Glacier Bay National Park. From here north, ice meets open ocean in bays fronting the St. Elias and Church mountains.

The outflow of vast icefields, the glaciers today give us some sense of what the entire coast (not to mention the continent), once looked like, some fifteen thousand years ago, as far south as the state of Washington. The last Ice Age buried the land, beneath ice several miles deep in some places. The tremendous eroding power of these massive glaciers trenched out the valleys and etched gaps between the mountains to such depths that when the ice retreated, the sea rushed in, creating the fjords and channels that carve up the coast and split it into hundreds of islands.

The archipelago of the Queen Charlotte Islands was the only part of this section of coast which escaped being scraped clean by the glaciers. This served as an evolutionary nursery, a refuge for plants and animals which recolonized the barren land after the glaciers retreated.

North America's Pacific coast is a wilderness of contrasts. The ragged, dissected northern portion could scarcely be more different from the clean break between land and sea that characterizes the coast south from the Olympic Peninsula. A highway parallels the southern edge, and access from land to sea is easy. But for the British Columbia coast and the Alaska Panhandle, with its Alexander Archipelago, the natural barriers are so daunting, the potential road so circuitous, that no coastal road can be built. Boats or seaplanes provide limited access to scattered Indian villages, logging camps, fish-processing plants and solitary lighthouses.

In terms of climate, a more marked contrast between the two stretches of coast is also difficult to imagine. Some of the most benign, perpetually sunny weather to be found anywhere graces the Baja Peninsula. It is Mediterranean, rather than desert.

One can camp comfortably under the stars with just a light blanket; the proximity of a warm sea precludes the cold nights common to desert regions. By stark contrast, in the mountains above the Gulf of Alaska is a wasteland of perpetual ice—the most extensively glaciated terrain at this low altitude in the world. It is not so much cold along the coast here as it is interminably damp and dreary. Precipitation, rather than extreme cold, feeds these icefields. Inhabitants count themselves lucky if they see the sun once a week.

Striking contrasts are apparent not just between widely dispersed parts of the Pacific coast, but often within the same small stretches of shoreline. Sandy beaches and rocky headlands alternate in varying proportions. The coast of Oregon is especially noted for cliffs and jagged sea stacks alternating with miles of beach. In places, smooth beach and steep rock pinnacles intermingle. In other places the shore is undulating for long distances. One of the greatest examples of coastal dunes in the world, the Oregon Dunes, between Florence and Coos Bay, comprise forty miles of shifting sand, sometimes cresting into peaks over six hundred feet high. Precipices of higher bluffs rise above the north and south borders of the dunes.

Beyond its contrasts, North America's Pacific coast is a wilderness described by superlatives. A redwood tree stands 364 feet high in Redwood National Park, south of Orick—the tallest known member of the tallest species on earth. Chatham Strait and Lynn Canal Taiya Inlet together form a channel that stretches for 240 miles from the Pacific to Skagway. Alaska and British Columbia claim the longest and the deepest fjords in the world. Records for climate are also impressive. The world's heaviest snowfalls have graced areas not far inland from the coast. On the slopes of Mount Rainier, visible from Puget Sound, more than 100 feet of snow once fell in a single season.

Perhaps the most awesome aspect, however, the most striking landscape superlative of the Pacific wilderness, refers to the St. Elias Mountains, which meet the sea along the Gulf of Alaska. These are the most magnificent coastal mountains in the world. Nowhere else do mountains whose base rests essentially in tidewater reach such altitudes. Nowhere else on earth do peaks of such splendid height coalesce with icefields and glaciers of such vast extent.

Arguably the greatest of the coastal peaks is Mount St. Elias itself. From the Malaspina Glacier at sea level the land ascends to a sharp summit, more than 18,000 feet high. Even in the Himalayas, or nearby on Denali in Alaska, there is no significantly greater vertical continuity of ice and rock.

Different worlds, superlative worlds; the Pacific wilderness is exceptional in itself. And married to the entire length of this spectacular coast swells the world's greatest ocean.

RESTLESS SEA

Wild. Wilderness. The distinctions between the two blur in descriptions of the Pacific coast to suggest at once an untameable energy, and a remote, unspoiled domain. The Pacific coast is not everywhere wilderness. The stretch that harbors metropolises like Los Angeles, with its skyscrapers, freeways and omnipresent smog, is an extreme example of the cityscapes that interrupt and desecrate the coastal wilderness. But the coast is everywhere wild. Against even the most slick urban developments crashes the formidable and relentless force of the ocean.

Ever restless, ever in motion, the Pacific moves in waves, tides and currents. Onrushing white skirts of broken waves display the ocean's power most conspicuously. Even on calm days, there is a swell, often big enough to create seven-foot-tall breakers where it hits the shore. The swell may have been fed by ripples of some long-spent storm off the coast of Asia, nudged along by prevailing winds. Once set on course, waves can forge their way across thousands of miles of open ocean, creating a tremendous surf, even where there may not be the slightest breeze.

Often the wind finds the ideal direction for optimum impact against distant shores. The westerlies, part of the prevailing pattern of global air circulation, consistently sweep latitudes between 30 and 60 degrees, precisely the location of the Pacific coast above southern Baja. Twenty-foot waves commonly crash onto the land in winter, when the wind is stronger, during storms which last for days.

Waves are conceived in the brush of air across water. Their size is technically a function of wind speed, duration and fetch, the distance over which the wind is active. For a wind taking a flying run at the west coast of North America, the potential fetch is vast. From Japan, it is more than five thousand miles across the North Pacific to Oregon. In the world between, there is nothing to act as an obstacle to wave building, not a single island.

Against a coast that tends to be soft in its geology, waves work prodigiously. Within this century, the shore has been carved back in some places by a distance the length of a football field. Evidence abounds of the ocean's power, and man's tendency to underestimate it. Stretches of former coastal highway lie tilted and broken, with slabs of old pavement hanging over new cliff faces. Once-valuable oceanfront houses are abandoned with futile "for sale" signs on lawns that

OPPOSITE:
A tiny island framed by the Strait of Georgia,
off the Sunshine Coast of British Columbia, near
Sechelt.

crumble into the sea. Deterioration of dwellings is one problem man contends with; the swallowing up of property is another. The ocean perseveres.

Diurnal tides move the cutting edge of the waves rhythmically up and down. Twice in a twenty-four hour day, the water retreats to reveal a colorful mass of sea life that dwells in tide pools and clings to slick rocks. Twice a day the sea again inundates the beach and rock piles or sea stacks become islands once more.

The sculpted natural beauty of the land-water margin is the finest art of the waves: in feathered, curved beaches of fine sand, in natural stone arches, in long rock channels lined with swaying seaweed, in deep grottoes gouged from cliff faces. Near Florence, Oregon, is one of the most magnificent grottoes. Here, a multi-entrance chamber, two acres in extent and 125 feet high, shelters a sea-lion rookery, home to hundreds of the bellowing mammals in spring and summer.

Sea stacks reign over all the wave-hewn features of the coast. Most common from northern California to the Olympic Peninsula in Washington, these monuments mark where the old shore once held against the sea, not very long ago in geological time. They take various forms as rock blocks, slabs, pyramids and towers, sometimes stranded far offshore.

Tidal range is not extreme along most of the coast, perhaps five feet in southern California, not more than ten feet on the Pacific shore of Vancouver Island. The exceptions are intriguing. Cook Inlet in Alaska acts as a giant funnel, somewhat like the well-known Bay of Fundy on the Atlantic coast. Like the Bay of Fundy, it creates a tremendous tidal range—more than thirty feet in Turn-again Arm. But the tides of the Pacific are at their most impressive in terms of sheer velocity. Some coves in British Columbia have the fastest tidal currents in the world.

In British Columbia, and in the Alaska Panhandle, most of the coastline is a maze of fjords and channels, surrounded by mountains and sheltered from the waves of the open Pacific. Except for the navigational concern of where and when the tides turn, one could cruise these waterways for weeks without sensing that they were contiguous with the ocean. In places like Nakwakto, Seymour and Skookumchuck Narrows, a passage less than half a mile wide connects an arm of the sea with an extensive network of inlets totaling as much as a hundred miles in length. On an incoming tide, the flow through such narrows is rapid and treacherous; on an outgoing tide, the inlets swell like bloated reservoirs behind a burst dam—the constricted narrows can't allow water out fast enough to keep pace with the receding sea. The result, a whirlpool the size of a city block, is called a maelstrom.

Greatest of all the oceans, the Pacific covers an area larger than all of the earth's continents combined and occupies a volume—in comparison to the land above sea level—many times greater. In turn it is under the influence of an even larger ocean, the atmosphere, an ocean of air. The prevailing circulation of the atmosphere governs ocean currents, which are in turn affected by differences in water density and water temperature.

While waves, tides and tidal currents are manifestations of the sea's restless movements, greater currents slowly stir entire oceans. Waves and tides shape the malleable coastline, while invisible ocean currents, through their influence on global climate, shape entire continents.

The movement of currents in the North Pacific is clockwise. Pushed by easterlies which girdle the middle of the globe, the North Equatorial Current gathers warm waters which then curve north past Japan as the Kuroshio Current. This current in turn veers right, to cross the ocean again as the warm Alaska Current. Coastal Alaska, as a result, has mild, though very wet, winters, in contrast to the coasts of Russia or Labrador at comparable latitudes. The current from Japan has much the same moderating influence on the northwestern Pacific coast as the Gulf Stream does on Europe.

Paradoxically, the portion of the North Pacific Drift which splits south to become the California Current is cold. Complex fluid mechanics and the slope of the coast combine with the California Current to provoke an upwelling of cold water from deep below the surface. This cold current is responsible for the summer mists that frequent the California coast.

The Pacific is alive with movement in a global dance performed to various rhythms simultaneously: the slow waltz of great currents, the steady pulse of tides, the vigorous beat of waves against shore. Perhaps the wildness of the sea is most evocative when it is approached from land, through the wilderness. There are places, such as Cape Alva in Washington and Cape Scott in British Columbia, where it takes the better part of a day to trek through deep forest to land's end. A constant shush of distant waves, a steady sibilation of water lapping sand and rock, heightens the magic of approach through the trees. Arriving at the ocean is like reaching the summit of a mountain—one is never prepared for the sudden expanse of horizon.

A wild shore intimates the rhythms of our planet. Waves and currents are born of the wind. And the earth's rotation imbues the wind with its prevailing slant. The ebb and flow of tides are linked too with the earth's turning, and the pull of the sun and the moon. The rhythm of the Pacific Ocean is indeed a rhythm of the spheres, its shores intoning a wild symphony of wind, water and rock.

PRECEDING PAGES:
Dawn illuminates a tropical stretch of the Pacific off the tip of the Baja Peninsula, Mexico.

ABOVE:
A 250-foot-high hat stack is one of the best known of the numerous pinnacles that adorn the coastline at Cannon Beach, Oregon.

ABOVE:
Late afternoon, coastal heath near Ophir,
Oregon.

ABOVE:
In southern Oregon, the smooth mirror of a beach deserted by the receding tide reflects the reds, pinks and yellows of a Pacific sundown.

OPPOSITE:
Sunset from Sol Mar Beach near Cabo San Lucas in Baja California.

OPPOSITE:
A long exposure accentuates the misty effect of surf breaking around sharp rocks off the Baja Peninsula, Mexico.

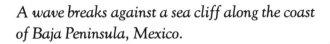

A wave breaks against a sea cliff along the coast of Baja Peninsula, Mexico.

At low tide on the Oregon coast, a glassy beach is strewn with rock piles.

PRECEDING PAGES:
*The shores of the Baja Peninsula near Cabo San
Lucas alternate between fine, sandy beaches and
sculpted cliffs.*

ABOVE:
*From this hill overlooking a beach in Olympic
National Park in California, sea stacks loom like
great sea beasts in the distance.*

OPPOSITE:
*The Pacific embraces a deserted beach near Todos
Santos on the Baja Peninsula, Mexico.*

A silvery stretch of the Pacific off Enderts Beach
in Redwood National Park, south of Crescent
City, California.

ABOVE:
Turnagain Arm in Alaska has the greatest tidal
range—thirty-three feet—on the Pacific coast.
Low tide leaves behind acres of mud flats contain-
ing treacherous pockets of quicksand.

OPPOSITE:
Across Cook Inlet from Anchorage, Alaska, the
Kenai Mountains rise above Turnagain Arm on a
summer evening.

ABOVE:
Jagged rocks and breaking surf—here softened by
a long exposure—are a common feature of the
coast between Santa Cruz and San Francisco.

ABOVE:
Low tide reveals stones slick with seaweed at the foot of Damnation Creek Trail in Del Norte Coast Redwoods State Park, California.

OPPOSITE:
Viewed from the southern end of Thrasher Cove, the shore along the West Coast trail in Pacific Rim National Park is mostly rocky and densely forested.

OPPOSITE:
Howe Sound is the first of scores of inlets north of Vancouver along the fjorded coast of British Columbia.

ABOVE:
Looking out from the mouth of Sea Lion Cave across Cape Cove, towards Heceta Head Lighthouse in Oregon.

PRECEDING PAGES:
Late afternoon sun silhouettes a pair of rocky islets against the shimmering Pacific, near Toleak Point in Olympic National Park, Washington.

OPPOSITE:
Near El Tule, Baja California, sandy beach is frequently interrupted by rocky outcrop.

ABOVE:
This picturesque grouping of sea stacks in Samuel H. Boardman State Park attests to the art of the Oregon waves.

OPPOSITE:
*Sunset illuminates low tide from the southern
end of Long Beach, Pacific Rim National Park,
British Columbia.*

ABOVE:
*Near Pistol River, Oregon, Route 101 provides
views of one spectacular bay after another.*

ABOVE:
Rocky headlands on a rainy day, Vancouver Island, British Columbia.

OPPOSITE:
The wave-hewn coast near Rockport, north of San Francisco on Highway 1.

Evening settles over Howe Sound near Brittania Beach, British Columbia.

Looking north from the inside passage between Vancouver Island and the mainland, British Columbia.

Fuchsia dusk near the California border in Oregon.

OPPOSITE:
*Sunset burnishes a small cove north of Chesterman
Beach near Tofino on Vancouver Island, British
Columbia.*

ABOVE:
*Cape Scott on Vancouver Island, British
Columbia.*

45

ABOVE:
At low tide, sea stacks tower over the Second Beach at Olympic National Park, Washington, like ancient fortresses.

OPPOSITE:
A tranquil tide pool is temporarily spared the on-slaught of surf on a rocky platform near Nels Bight at the north end of Vancouver Island, British Columbia.

OPPOSITE:
An offshore mist darkens the sky as cords of break-
ers crash on the wide beach at Nels Bight, northern
Vancouver Island, British Columbia.

ABOVE:
Strong winds sweeping Hecate Strait create frothy
breakers near Tlell on Graham Island in the
Queen Charlottes, British Columbia.

ABOVE:
Here, a day's hike from the nearest road, most of
the coast in Olympic National Park is a wilderness of sea stacks and rocky inlets.

OPPOSITE:
Surf pounds Cape Scott, the northwesternmost tip
of Vancouver Island, British Columbia.

50

SUSPECT TERRAIN

Land changes, but usually so slowly that it appears unaltered over the course of a human lifetime. The Grand Canyon gets deeper, the Himalayas grow taller. But land exposed to the erosion of the sea is an exception: an entire beach may be moved by a single storm, or several feet might be chopped from a soft escarpment where, a mile back from shore, the terrain appears solid and secure.

Along the Pacific coast, at irregular though not infrequent intervals, there have been catastrophic reminders that *terra firma* is not all it appears to be.

Seven hundred people died and a quarter of a million were left homeless in San Francisco, on April 18, 1906, after earthquake and fire destroyed much of what was then the largest town in the west. The city had jumped twenty feet north relative to the rest of the continent.

On July 9, 1958, a colossal wave swept a forest and, incidentally, three fishing boats out to sea after a landslide crashed into the head of Lituya Bay, Alaska. Ninety million tons of rock fell from the Fairweather Range, smashed half a mile off the end of a tidewater glacier, and thrust up a wall of water that, on one mountainside, reached a height of two thousand feet. An earthquake triggered the event, as the terrain on the seaward side of the Fairweather fault lurched eight yards north. (Miraculously, the crews of two of the boats survived.)

The most severe earthquake in North America in this century struck Alaska on March 27, 1964, killing more than a hundred people and changing the level of fifty thousand square miles of land. Seismic sea waves from the quake drowned a dozen people in northern California.

At Mount St. Helens, Washington, more than half a cubic mile of crushed and molten rock exploded from the once-sleeping volcano, destroying an area of two hundred square miles and killing sixty-seven people on May 18, 1980. St. Helens is one of a string of volcanoes in the Cascade Mountains, many of which can be seen from the coast.

These episodes are particularly significant only because they happened in this century and have been well documented. Hundreds, even thousands, of other violent earthquakes have disturbed Alaska and California. One in 1858 south of San Francisco was considerably more severe than the one which destroyed the city. Many great waves have roared down the course of Lituya Bay.

OPPOSITE:
White cloud fills the Hoh Valley of Mount Olympus in Olympic National Park, Washington.

In terms of geological history, moreover, these events have happened more or less simultaneously. A century is of less significance in the life of the Earth than a minute is in a human lifetime.

The land along the Pacific coast is much more active and violent than that in the center of the continent or along the east coast. The reasons for this were not entirely clear until the last two decades, when studies were made of rock taken from many miles down in the Pacific. While historically it had been believed that the rock in the ocean basins must be ancient, these studies established that exactly the opposite was the case: nowhere within the floor of the ocean could rock be found that was more than 160 million years old, ie., less than one-twentieth as old as the oldest rocks discovered on the continents.

This data fit in neatly with the theory of plate tectonics, which holds that the earth's crust consists of a number of rigid plates "floating" on a hot, solid but plastic mantle, and that these plates have drifted considerable distances around the surface of the planet. Since the crust is solid rock virtually everywhere around the globe, including under the oceans, the only way that it can move is by parts of it riding over other parts, which disappear below the surface as new parts appear elsewhere. This happens primarily to the dense rock of the ocean floor, and explains its relatively young age: it is constantly being recycled, somewhat like the upper surface of a conveyor belt.

We need to grasp what is happening more than six thousand miles away in the Atlantic to understand fully the landscape of the Pacific coast. There, a great mountain-banked crack in the bottom, the Mid-Atlantic Ridge, is growing wider, and molten lava is pouring out, laying down new ocean floor as the Atlantic widens. This rift opened 140 million years ago when there was only one major continent, Pangea, and only one ocean, Panthalassa. With the split-up of the supercontinent and the birth of the Atlantic, the portion that is now North America moved westward.

The east side of North America is known in geological terms as a passive margin. It and the adjacent western Atlantic basins are an integral unit, parts of the North American Plate, moving away together from the Eurasian and African Plates. The Pacific side, by contrast, is an active margin. Here the North American Plate is crashing into other plates, including the eastward-moving and now nearly extinct Farallon Plate, resulting in a continuous series of tremendous geological events, minor manifestations of which are the death-dealing earthquakes and volcanoes.

The character of the Pacific coast is a product of these events, of subduction and suspect terrain. "Subduction" is the earth scientist's term for what must happen when two plates, two vast areas of the earth's surface, or lithosphere, collide. When the edge of a continent collides with the edge of oceanic litho-sphere, as has happened along the Pacific coast, something has to give, and the plate with the denser basalt rock of the ocean basin inevitably dives under the lighter granitic rock of the continent. It is then absorbed into the hot mantle of the earth, from which it originally came.

Subduction produces great heat, which melts rock and produces the liquid magma that, rising to the surface, creates volcanoes. The molten rock that prompted the eruption of Mount St. Helens was formed by the slow but massive dive of the Juan de Fuca Plate (the remains of the Farallon Plate), under the continental shelf a hundred miles off the coast of Washington and Oregon. (The push and drag of the same plate created the Olympic Mountains.) The Aleutian Islands consist of volcanoes which have erupted north of the arc where the Pacific Plate is plunging under the North American Plate off Alaska. Stresses created from the subduction of this same plate caused the Alaska Earthquake.

The entire Pacific coast, together with most of the Western Cordillera, consists of some fifty different pieces of the earth's surface which geologists define as "suspect terrain," a fascinating mystery whose solution has only recently been recognized. The volcanoes are made of the only rock near the Pacific coast which sits, relative to the continent as a whole, where it was originally formed. The rest, including land as far from the ocean as parts of Idaho, Nevada and northern Alaska, was not originally part of North America.

The terrains are called suspect because they emigrated from other, sometimes unknown, positions on the globe. Islands and micro-continents piled up against the western margin of North America and stuck there while the surrounding ocean floor disappeared into the earth's interior. The collision of these land masses lifted rugged mountains, nowhere more dramatically than in the Wrangell and St. Elias ranges, where the southwest corner of the Yukon today elbows into Alaska. The stone in these high, ice-bound peaks came from a micro-continent called Wrangellia, which once lay near the equator. Vancouver Island and the Queen Charlotte Islands are also remnants of that broken prehistoric land.

Bits and pieces from numerous other vanished lands have made the west coast a geological melting pot where virtually every landscape is an alien. The great earth movements responsible for this assembly continue their work. Baja and part of California south of Point Reyes are heaving up the coast in jerky steps along the San Andreas Fault. It is a popular belief that, with one massive shrug of the earth, the most populous part of California will one day collapse into the sea. The earthquakes serve as reminders of the movement of plates, a process that over the last two hundred million years has contributed land to this margin of the continent. The land, like the wind, has arrived from the west, from across the ocean. Pacific waves once beat against rocks which are now three hundred miles east of the shore.

PRECEDING PAGES:
Sun bakes the flanks of a sea cliff near Cabo San Lucas in Baja California.

OPPOSITE:
The moon glows through a crevice in rock cliffs near the southernmost tip of the Baja Peninsula, Mexico.

ABOVE:
A gently curved line of sandstone conglomerate, part of an intriguing rockscape at Point Lobos State Reserve near Carmel, California.

ABOVE:
Pacific dogwood blossoms across the river banks in Stamp Falls Provincial Park on Vancouver Island, British Columbia.

OPPOSITE:
An azure evening sea viewed from a shell-covered beach on Galiano Island, one of the Gulf Islands of British Columbia.

PRECEDING PAGES:
A backpacker pauses at the mouth of an Owen Point sea cave in the Pacific Rim National Park, British Columbia.

ABOVE:
Sea stacks in an evening drizzle are mirrored by the beach near Quateata in Olympic National Park, south of La Push.

OPPOSITE:
In the Coast mountains near Stewart, British Columbia, the Bear Glacier descends almost to sea level.

PRECEDING PAGES:
*Advancing waves of sand overrun the skeletons of
doomed trees in the Oregon Dunes, near Florence.*

OPPOSITE:
*A coastal trail in Olympic National Park skirts
this waterfall on Goodman Creek.*

ABOVE:
*Near Fredericksen Point, Vancouver Island. Like
giant flowerpots, many eroded rocks off the coast
of British Columbia support solitary trees.*

OPPOSITE:
Spirited waterfalls plunge through the mountain-walled inlets of the British Columbia and Alaska coasts.

ABOVE:
Glaciers and spring flowers engulf the mountain valleys along Alaska's coast. The Byron Glacier near Anchorage is one of the most accessible.

OPPOSITE:
*Like immense abstract sculptures, sensual rock
forms are bathed in the afterglow of sundown near
Cabo San Lucas, Baja California.*

ABOVE:
*A purple dusk settles over Discovery Passage
off Vancouver Island, British Columbia.*

PRECEDING PAGES:
A view of the Coast Mountains beyond Squamish at the head of Howe Sound, British Columbia.

OPPOSITE:
Late afternoon light bounces off the waters of Pender Harbor near Madeira Park, British Columbia.

ABOVE:
The predominantly sandstone shores of the gulf islands in the Strait of Georgia, British Columbia, are noted for strange formations indicative of this "suspect" terrain.

OPPOSITE:
A *fingernail moon hangs over sea stacks north of Cape Ferrelo, Oregon.*

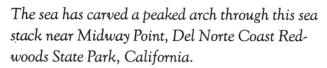

The sea has carved a peaked arch through this sea stack near Midway Point, Del Norte Coast Redwoods State Park, California.

Shannon Falls tumbles down a cliff face, near Squamish, British Columbia.

Hearty grasses, some of them introduced, are stabilizing and curbing the natural drift of the Oregon Dunes.

Near Guise Bay in Cape Scott Provincial Park,
Vancouver Island, sun-bleached trees surrender
to shifting dunes.

The Oregon Dunes stretch for forty miles between
Florence and Coos Bay.

PRECEDING PAGES:
On a stretch of the Baja coast in late afternoon, the sunlit cliff is rough-hewn, while the rock in the foreground has been polished smooth by waves.

The Stamp River troughs and winds its way through the mountainous and densely forested interior of Vancouver Island.

OVERLEAF:
*Glaciers encrust the Chugach Mountains
in Alaska.*

*The Kenai Mountains from Moose Pass, about
midway across the Kenai Peninsula, Alaska.*

OPPOSITE:
*Tumultous surf, rock and forest fuse at
Long Beach, Pacific Rim National Park,
British Columbia.*

ABOVE:
*Mossy terrain embanks a gorge in the Qualicum
Park on Vancouver Island.*

OVERLEAF:
*Growlers and bergy bits, the smaller pieces of ice
calved from a parent glacier, bob at the foot of
Holgate Glacier where it spills into the Kenai
Fjord, Alaska.*

PRECEDING PAGES:
Kamishak Bay, where the McNeil River flows into Alaska.

ABOVE:
Clouds of mist drift in the hills above San Francisco in this early morning view from Mount Tamalpais.

ABOVE:
Not far from the head of Cook Inlet in
Alaska, the Portage Glacier calves icebergs
into Portage Lake.

OVERLEAF:
Lowell Glacier is one aspect of the world's largest
concentration of icefields and glaciers dominating
Kluane National Park, Yukon Territory.

OPPOSITE:
Mist contours a hilly stretch of coastline north of San Francisco, California.

ABOVE:
Dense forests maintain a tenuous foothold on the steep, rocky edges of the British Columbia coast.

REDWOODS AND SALMON

A rattlesnake winds its way across the sandy top of a Baja beach. Mountain goats descend to sea level for respite from a heavy winter snowfall. Deer, cougars and bears hide in the rainforest. Kittiwakes cement their nests to the edges of ocean cliffs. Life in the desert, life in the forest, life in the mountains and the rivers, life in tide pools and in the open sea—the full range of flora and fauna in the wilderness hugging the Pacific coast is extraordinarily rich and varied.

The land animals that populate the Pacific wilderness are not, for the most part, peculiar to the Pacific margin. Their kind may range far across the North American continent. There are, however, exceptions, whole races or subspecies that have become identified with the coast. The Roosevelt elk, significant numbers of which live among the redwoods of Olympic National Park, is one example. The mountain beaver, a tunnel-building burrower rather than a dam builder, not really a beaver and not confined to mountains, is another. The Columbian blacktail deer, a subspecies of the mule deer, is to be found only in the forested coastal regions of the Pacific, from Central California to southern British Columbia. The Kodiak bear of Alaska, once considered distinct and now classified as a subspecies of grizzly, is as evocative of the Pacific wilderness as the salmon it spends so much of its time pursuing.

By supporting isolated breeding populations, islands provide ideal conditions for the evolution of new species. Different races of deer, rodents and black bear have evolved on the islands fringing the Pacific coast. Vancouver Island, for example, has fostered the Vancouver Island marmot, a harmless, endearing creature with a coat whose color varies seasonally from black through cinnamon. Once numerous, its population today is estimated at less than one hundred. It is believed to be a descendant of the more common hoary marmot, but how it got to the island is a matter of conjecture. Many other animals common to the mainland opposite, such as mountain goats, porcupines and grizzlies, are absent from Vancouver Island. One plausible theory is that it was introduced by coastal Indians.

Plant life tends to be more firmly rooted to terrain and climate. The great trees, reigned over by the coast redwoods, are the Pacific coast's most prominent flora. They grow nowhere else in the world except in a narrow strip along the coast of California and southernmost Oregon. Thirty miles inland, beyond the reach of ocean mists, the redwoods disappear.

OPPOSITE:
*Ferns completely cover the sheer walls of Fern
Canyon, a fifty-foot-deep gorge on Home Creek
in Prairie Creek Redwoods Park, California.*

Tallest of the trees after the redwood is the coastal variety of Douglas fir. There is some evidence to suggest that individual trees felled by loggers near Vancouver once exceeded four hundred feet in length. Douglas firs might have once reached heights to compete with the tallest known redwoods.

Another giant is the Sitka spruce, which lives near the sea. It mingles with redwoods in northern California and ranges far into Alaska. The largest known specimen, near Cannon beach in Oregon, is 216 feet tall, but has a circumference of fifty-two feet, comparable to that of the most imposing redwoods.

Other unique trees are also encouraged by the coastal climate. They make up in beauty and character what they lack in size: the arbutus, the Pacific dogwood, the bigleaf maple, the California laurel (or the Oregon myrtle, depending on which state you are in), and the very rare and restricted Monterey cypress. By contrast, the scattered vegetation and wildlife of the 450-mile long Baja Peninsula represent an ecosystem that is independent of the sea's influence.

The desert community of plants is yet another of the remarkable and different worlds that exist adjacent to the Pacific. Here thrive the brilliant and the bizarre: muscular, wrinkled elephant trees; spindly thorn-mantled canes of ocotillo; tapered, drooping boojums; tall, erect and stately cardon cactii, daggered rosettes of yucca and once-in-a-lifetime blooming agaves. Eagles rest in resplendent palms lining oases and saltwater lagoons.

Most astonishing, perhaps, is the waterbound life that flourishes in the Pacific. In the intertidal zone, on temporarily exposed rocks or in tide pools dwell some of the sea's most primitive and exotic animals: multi-hued sea stars, anemones, sea urchins, barnacles, mussels, clams, abalone and crabs. And the shallow waters of just offshore host many thousands of invertebrates, seaweeds and fishes, many of them unique to their locale.

Whole colonies of birds depend on the smaller fishes of the sea. Pelicans, cormorants, puffins, murres, the ubiquitous gulls, the occasional heron stalking its prey from a raft of kelp, and many others. But few creatures have so poignant a lifecycle, or figure so centrally in the ecosystem of a region, as the Pacific salmon. The salmon serve as a primary food source for bears, eagles and some seals, to name a few of its followers. All the various species of salmon live as adults in the ocean, ultimately returning long distances upstream in the rivers where they were born, to spawn and to die.

There are few species in the open sea which belong only to the Pacific coast of North America. These include most of the great marine mammals—whales, dolphins and porpoises—the creatures that come first to mind when we think of ocean life. Two marine animals, however, are especially associated with this coast. The grey whales migrate every winter from Alaska to warm and sheltered bays in Baja to give birth to their young, notably to the Scammons and San

Ignacio lagoons. Once nearing extinction, the grey whale is making a gradual comeback, and the sight of its spout is an experience unique to the west coast.

The other whale—more properly a large dolphin—that has come to be associated with this coast is the orca, or killer whale. Although it can live as far away as Antarctica, the greatest numbers can be observed cruising in family groups, called pods, in inland waterways between Vancouver Island and the mainland.

Of marine mammals which retain links with the land, seven species frequent the west coast from the Aleutians southward. The sea otter is the smallest, and even it can weigh as much as a hundred pounds. Its coat of a billion very fine hairs traps air to make the animal buoyant. It is known for its habit of floating on its back and devouring its catch—clams, mussels, abalone—by cracking their shells open on a rock which it holds on its chest. The sea otter also likes to eat sea urchins—morsels for which it doesn't need the rock.

Seals and sea lions, or pinnipeds, make up the remaining half dozen species. They are generally classified into two groups, true seals and eared seals. The gregarious eared seals include the Guadeloupe fur seal, the California sea lion and Steller's sea lion. With deep-voiced bulls weighing as much as half a ton, Steller's sea lion is the largest of the group. Of the true seals, the harbor seal is smallest. The northern elephant seal, sometimes weighing two tons, is still a swift and graceful swimmer.

Pinnipeds share common breeding patterns. The males haul out on the rocks first and stake out territories. The females follow, give birth and breed again not long afterwards. Apart from breeding, pinnipeds are completely at home in the water. Some species can dive to depths of two thousand feet and stay under water for up to forty-five minutes. After weaning, northern fur seal pups spend their first few years on their own out in the open ocean, without ever returning to land until they are ready to mate.

Popular with hunters, and unpopular with the fishermen whose nets they pirate, three species of these marvelous mammals were within a hair of becoming extinct: the sea otter, the Guadeloupe fur seal and the northern elephant seal. Their numbers are now relatively secure but only by some luck were they saved. Man's care for the living heritage of the Pacific wilderness has been less than commendable. Nowhere in Canada, that country so identified with wilderness, is a significant stand of coastal rainforest likely to survive in its impressive, primeval state into the next century. Some of America's greatest forests have been treated with more foresight, but all the centuries-old trees including the rare Port Orford cedar, are being eliminated much faster than they are being regenerated. The so-called "redwood empire" is sadly an empire no more, just patches of small parks marking where once-grand forests grew. As awesome as the life of the Pacific wilderness remains, it is vulnerable.

ABOVE:
Bigleaf maple and alder are hardwoods common to moss-sheathed rainforests from southern British Columbia to California.

OPPOSITE:
The Douglas fir and the western hemlock are two of the largest species reigning in the rainforests of Washington.

ABOVE:
*Stonecrop is a succulent common to the sandstone
shores of the Gulf Islands in British Columbia and
the adjacent San Juan Islands in Washington.*

OPPOSITE:
*Lupine thrives in the Oregon Dunes, here near
Suislaw River.*

Inside the sea lion cave, Oregon, two sea lions
recline beside the surging surf.

Guillemots, in the sea cliffs along the
Oregon coast.

OPPOSITE:
A pair of herring gulls are reflected in
the calm inland waters off Gabriola Island,
British Columbia.

PRECEDING PAGES:
Club mosses envelope a bigleaf maple in the dense forest of Vancouver Island.

OPPOSITE:
Detail of colorful bark of the arbutus, or Pacific madrone, which ranges along the coast from California to southern British Columbia.

ABOVE:
Redwood trees, pillars of the forest, British Columbia.

Striped like a chipmunk except for its face, the golden-mantled ground squirrel is sometimes known as the "golden chipmunk."

ABOVE:
Exhausted after a round of playful sparring,
black bear cubs rest in a fallen big-leaf maple.

OVERLEAF:
Steller's sea lions congregate noisily at Cape St.
James, on the southern tip of the Queen Charlotte
Islands, British Columbia.

OPPOSITE:
*Popular with browsing deer and bear despite its
pungent odor, the skunk cabbage flowers in spring, in
the wet forests and swamplands of British Columbia.*

ABOVE:
*Patches of color in the undergrowth brighten a
coastal forest in autumn.*

OPPOSITE:
An *arbutus tree in spring bloom clings to the steep shore overlooking Saanich Inlet near Victoria, British Columbia.*

ABOVE:
Detail of a beach composed entirely of bits of shell, on Galiano Island, British Columbia.

121

OPPOSITE:
Cormorants fish from an islet dwarfed by Mount Augustine, a sometimes-active volcano, in Alaska.

ABOVE:
Traveling in family groups called pods, orcas, or killer whales, range all over the globe but are frequently sighted off the coasts of Washington and British Columbia.

OPPOSITE:
Smallest of the pinnipeds, harbor seals feed on smaller marine animals and salmon, diving as deep as 300 feet for their prey.

ABOVE:
Elephant seal bulls stage bellowing duels to establish dominance over their breeding territories.

PRECEDING PAGES:
Gathering annually along a 100-yard stretch of rapids, as many as eighty bears, and innumerable gulls, share the plenty of the salmon run in July and August at McNeil River, Alaska.

ABOVE:
Foliage overlooking the Oregon coast.

Fireweed thrives in a variety of habitats, here amidst young fir trees at the top of a remote, misty beach on Vancouver Island, British Columbia.

Multi-hued sea stars of all kinds share a beach in the Burnaby Narrows, Queen Charlotte Islands, British Columbia.

Sea stars proliferate in tide pools along the shores of the sheltered islands between British Columbia and the State of Washington.

Sea anemone, exposed in its tidepool, on the Washington coast.

OPPOSITE:
Forests of red alder range from California to Alaska.

ABOVE:
Thousands of colossal, moss-draped trunks loom above the Miners Ridge Trail in Prairie Creek Redwoods State Park, California.

OPPOSITE:
A suspicious porcupine displays its quills.

ABOVE:
Known for its shrill whistle, the hoary marmot protects itself from predators by burrowing under boulders; this one is hiding from a coyote.

OPPOSITE:
In spring, flowering Pacific dogwood ranges from central California to southern British Columbia.

Latticed, moss-covered branches of an aging red alder near Port Clements on Graham Island in the Queen Charlottes, British Columbia.

Moss carpets the rainforest floor on the Queen Charlotte Islands, British Columbia.

PRECEDING PAGES:
Scavenging sea gulls inundate a glistening low-tide beach near Netarts on the Oregon coast.

ABOVE:
Kittiwakes build their nests in high ocean cliffs, coming ashore only to breed.

OPPOSITE:
A young bald eagle, sated with feeding on exhausted salmon during the spawning season in Alaska.

PHOTO CREDITS

Fred Bruemmer, 124, 125
Fraser Clark, 79 (below), 116-117, 130
Thomas Kitchin (First Light), 88, 115, 134
Brian Milne (First Light), 139
Pat Morrow (First Light), 99
James Page, 135
Leanna Rath, 114, 118, 119
Robert Semeniuk (First Light), 21 (above), 98
Karl Sommerer, 90-91, 92-93, 122, 126-127, 128, 131 (right), 142, 143
Peter Thomas, 123
Ole Westby, 113 (right)

All other photographs by J.A. Kraulis.

Front cover:
Experiment Bight in Cape Scott Provincial Park, British Columbia.

Back cover:
View of the Kenai Mountains from Moose Pass, about midway across the Kenai
Peninsula, Alaska.